Learning Decoded

Understanding and Using Your Child's Unique Learning Style to Improve Academic Performance

By Heather Leneau Bragg

With Patricia Alma Lee

Published by Hypethral Publishing, Chicago, IL

ISBN 978-0-9889776-0-0
LCCN 2013902507

DISCLAIMER

This book is not intended for use in diagnosing
children with learning disabilities or any other psychological or
medical condition, nor is this book a substitute for neurological,
neuropsychological or psychoeducational evaluation and treatment.
I encourage parents of children with learning difficulties to
pursue an evaluation with a licensed professional.

To Aaron

It was through becoming a parent myself that
I first felt the desire to gather every resource imaginable
to prepare myself to guide you through this beautiful
and challenging journey called life.

Acknowledgments

To my parents, Harry and Judy Leneau, who not only encouraged me to pursue my passions and be an independent thinker, they also paid for my education.

To my coauthor Pat Alma Lee, whose professional advice and personal support and enthusiasm made this project possible.

To Steve Pavilonis, who blazed this writing trail before me and was my Yoda for being an author.

To Phil Bellagamba, for his professional advice.

To Kristen Coffman, who remains the best teacher I have ever seen, even after fifteen years in the field. I wish my son could have you as a teacher!

To the College of Education at the University of Oklahoma, especially Dr. Sally Beach and Dr. Neil Hauser. My experiences with both of you guide me daily.

To the Department of Communication Sciences and Disorders at Northwestern University, especially Dr. Steve Zecker and Frank Van Santen, who continually answer my out-of-the-blue email questions.

To Mandy Bunte, whose leadership skills and calm demeanor with challenging students served as a wonderful example of patience and thoughtful teaching.

To Mike Taback, who taught me about math instruction.

To Kristy Marling, who taught me about science instruction.

To Teresa Deckert Taylor, another fantastic teacher from whom I learned so much.

To Allana Bourne for her editing.

Foreword

Studies examining the prevalence rates of developmental disabilities and psychiatric conditions in children in the last two decades demonstrate a consistent increase. Reasons for this are not completely clear, however we know that we are better at recognizing and diagnosing the conditions which may play a significant role. The obstacles children face in learning are significant. For example, a study in July of 2010, cited that approximately one in five children exhibit a psychiatric disorder with impairment upon formal schooling. In addition to this, Centers for Disease Control data reports that the rates of any developmental disability (including both learning disabilities and Attention Deficit Hyperactivity Disorder, abbreviated ADHD) are 13.9% in the U.S. Furthermore, we are facing an ever increasing prevalence of Autism Spectrum Disorders, which the CDC is currently approximating to be 1/88 children. So whatever the cause or diagnosis, we know that children have many obstacles to learning by the time they hit kindergarten.

Schools are then faced with the ever increasing challenge of meeting each individual child's academic needs. Parents are faced with trying to understand their child's needs and then negotiating them with the school system. In my experience, this is overwhelming for most parents.

In "Learning, Decoded: Understanding and Using Your Child's Unique Learning Style to Improve Academic Performance," author Heather Bragg, MA, graduate of Northwestern University, transforms her brilliant neurocognitive knowledge base of learning disorders into a practical guide for parents. Heather has a unique ability and enthusiasm to understand and creatively approach each individual child's academic and learning needs, which is evident in her writing and the suggestions/examples outlined in this book.

In my experience in working with children and families with special needs, many parents and children end up feeling frustrated and exasperated unnecessarily, as a better understanding of the obstacles they are facing and how to problem-solve around them would alleviate much of their distress. This book outlines a modern, practical way to understand learning disabilities and offers suggestions to help parents and children get what they need out of their educational experience. This is a must read for any parent who has a child struggling in school.

—Jennifer Kurth, DO

Assistant Professor, Northwestern University Feinberg
School of Medicine, Department of Psychiatry and Behavioral
Neurosciences, Division of Child and Adolescent Psychiatry,
Attending Physician and Director of Education, Child and
Adolescent Fellowship Training Director, Ann and Robert H.
Lurie Children's Hospital of Chicago, Department of Child and
Adolescent Psychiatry

Contents

Introduction

I had no idea how to help Anthony then.

I was teaching first grade on Chicago's West Side. A student of mine—we'll call him Anthony—was not learning to read. He could not sound out three-letter words like "cat." He knew all of the letters of the alphabet and their corresponding sounds, but, faced with more than one letter in a row, he did not know what to do or say. I was so frustrated with myself. What had worked for my other students hadn't for him, for example, working with rhymes and words with the same initial letter and sound, and manipulating sounds (For example, "Say the word 'dog' without the /d/"). Although I had a bachelor's degree in elementary education and had completed graduate courses in reading instruction, this child's problem had me baffled. I had even read all of the "hot" books in the field of reading instruction and literacy. Yet I was still stumped. He and I worked together for many hours before and after school, trying to make some progress. With his big round eyes and quiet demeanor, Anthony seemed unfazed by his lack of progress. I may have appeared calm and encouraging on the outside, but inside I was panicking. If Anthony didn't learn to read soon, he would start down the path many children take—falling a little behind, then farther behind, and then resenting school, and finally, turned off to learning. He had no inkling of the gravity of the situation. But I did, and I felt paralyzed as I watched the unhappy cycle begin.

A few years later, after completing a master's degree and getting additional training, I thought back to Anthony's struggle. What a shame that I hadn't been able to help him then. Now that I have acquired more tools, I can use my additional training and experience. Can I help him now? I believe I can.

More students than ever are falling behind in our schools and school systems are not any closer to finding ways to help them. While the media has highlighted the subject of school reform—thanks to books and documentaries released recently—financial cutbacks and funding problems undermine the momentum toward significant change. To better meet a child's needs, teachers and parents need a good understanding of recent brain-based research findings.

The purpose of this book is to empower parents and other teachers to act on behalf of the many children who struggle in school. Parents are often the best teachers and can contribute to their child's success when they know what to do. My vision is that teachers and parents need to work together much earlier to understand and address learning issues. My goal is to explain how learning happens as clearly and concisely as possible in order to help teachers, students and their families to understand how best to accurately assess the complicated process of learning to teach/learn/adapt instruction.

Learning Decoded: Understanding and Using Your Child's Unique Learning Style to Improve Academic Performance is meant to be clear and reader-friendly. I explain terms used in clinical and research materials so that you may benefit from them. They will probably be part of the language you hear as you help children. When discussing a child's learning issues, I most often refer to the child as "he." I have a son and am writing from the perspective of both teacher and parent. Also, using one pronoun is much simpler! Please be aware that any child discussed has had his name and identifying details changed for privacy.

How to Use this Book

I wrote this book with the struggling pupil in mind and my experience centers on children with as-yet undiagnosed learning disabilities and diagnosed mild-to-moderate learning disabilities. Look in the Appendix for resources for parents and teachers whose children are older or have additional complications such as severe cognitive and/or physical handicaps, hearing and/or vision deficits, behavior and emotional disorders.

First, let me define the term "learning disability," as it is often misunderstood and misused. A learning disability is a medical diagnosis and can be found in the Diagnostic & Statistical Manual of Mental Disorders (DSM-5). This is the medical manual of mental conditions that categorizes all official diagnoses published by the American Psychiatric Association. An evaluation by a qualified professional, such as a neuropsychologist or clinical psychologist, is necessary when diagnosing a learning disability. A child who has a medically diagnosed learning disability is one who has average to above-average cognitive abilities (intelligence quotient or IQ) and one or more processing deficits that disrupt his ability to perform in a way that matches his intelligence. In other words, he is a perfectly intelligent child who has some inconsistency in brain function that negatively affects school performance.

We all have our strengths and weaknesses. In a child with a learning disability, however, the gap between his areas of strength and weakness is more dramatic. Have you ever known someone who was exceptional at one thing and not so good— even terrible!—at another? You probably have. You may have wondered how this smart person could have such a disparity. For instance, I have a friend who is a mechanical engineer but cannot spell. If her intelligence was measured by her spelling ability alone, she would be judged as significantly less smart than she really is. Likewise, students with a specific learning disability have one or more specific problems sabotaging their ability to show how much they know and what they can do.

We are each unique. Ideally, the way our brains work is compatible with the way we are taught and the way we are asked to demonstrate our knowledge. But this is not always the case. To figure out where your child's learning challenges are, this book will help you look at **input** (the way information comes into the brain), **brain processes** (the aspects of learning needed for this specific activity) and **output** (how the student shows what he knows). By breaking your child's learning tasks into these pieces, you can begin to figure out why he struggles in school, as well as how to help. As I stated above, that is the purpose of this book.

Tremendous progress is being made in the fields of psychology, neuroscience and education. However, if you ask any two professionals in these fields about their theories of learning, you will probably hear different answers. There is still so much we do not know, and since every child is an individual and every brain is mysterious, it is understandable why debate exists. This book reflects my current understanding of learning and supporting struggling students.

I encourage anyone who finds this book helpful to continue studying about learning and cognition. Please review the resource list of books and other materials in the Appendix for ideas about what to study.

I have lots of ideas and ways to help a challenged learner like Anthony now. My goal is that, after you read this book, you will too.

How This Book is Organized

This book includes information from many sources, as well as my personal experiences as a general classroom and learning disabilities teacher. It is published as a specific reference and resource for parents and educators who are informally and formally teaching children struggling in pre-school and elementary grades first through fourth. This book provides a framework for the following.

1. Understanding input, or how information is being communicated to the student. Is he learning by listening to the teacher talk? From reading a book? From a chart?

2. Understanding brain processing abilities, such as the attention, memory, organization and visual spatial reasoning needed to master an assignment or task.

3. Understanding output, or the expectation for how the student should respond to successfully complete the task. Does he need to write a book report? Answer questions on a test? Complete math problems? Build a model?

4. Dissecting academic tasks according to input, processing and output and using this structure to determine where a breakdown in learning is occurring. Maybe the student doesn't understand the information when it is being taught? Or maybe it is hard for him to pay attention so he can remember it? Is it possible that he understood everything, his brain made sense of it and stored it well, but he still finds it difficult to write those spellings words during the test, conduct that science experiment or give a talk about the book he read?

5. Implementing a plan to work with and around challenging areas to help the student succeed. And last, using the plan to aid the student in understanding himself, his learning preferences and how to best use his strengths.

In my explanations, I primarily use layman's terms. Please remember that the brain processes being discussed (memory, attention, etc.) work closely together even though I discuss each aspect separately. Getting a feel for the complicated processes of learning is most important for our purposes. Grasping their intricacies and becoming an expert isn't necessary. (You can spend a lifetime learning about learning. Many people do just that!) Once you understand more about learning, you get a better idea of what is specifically going on with a child and can make more targeted attempts to help him.

Discussing how and why students struggle in pre-school and school is often a taboo subject. The current climate, while well-intentioned in its focus on sensitivity, can limit a teacher's ability to accurately describe students' challenges. My view is that clearly and accurately discussing individual differences can move toward an honest, yet equally sensitive, discussion that serves to support and benefit the student. It is not useful to talk around the problems or pretend that "everything will work out with time." Outright denial of a child's learning challenges also denies him the help he needs to succeed. Struggling students and their families must know that they are not alone. They can empower themselves and their children by taking an active part in their children's education.

Throughout this book, you will read the phrase "cognitive ability," and I would like to define that here. This is a person's intellectual ability or intelligence. We all have cognitive abilities that are part of our brains' make-up and these cannot be ignored when we discuss learning and academic performance.

Strengths and weaknesses, a normal part of every person, do not have to be worn as a label or a prediction of future success or failure. We each have abilities that are naturally stronger than others and these are more readily recognized and used.

On that note, measuring a person's intelligence is a complicated process. To measure accurately, a thorough psychoeducational evaluation needs to be conducted with your child by a clinical psychologist, however, at this point, there may be no need to shoulder the time and expense of a days-long testing session with your child which results in hard numbers. Instead, while reading this book, I suggest you use the knowledge you already have of your child to get a better idea of his intelligence without relying on an actual IQ or other testing score.

In addition to intelligence, I discuss cognitive processing in detail in the "Brain Processes" chapter of this book. Included are attention, memory, reasoning, executive functioning (organization) and many more. Each aspect greatly affects learning and school performance. For example, I have a good auditory memory. I remember what I have heard fairly accurately. However, I possess a so-so visual memory and so have more difficulty remembering what I have seen. No one is equally good in these processes. After I describe them in detail, I also discuss which most greatly influence success in math, reading, spelling, writing essays and other school-related tasks.

With new information on processing and the framework for evaluating academic tasks (input, output), you will be able to make a more targeted attempt to help your child. I also list and describe helpful stategies and methods of teaching throughout the book and in the Appendix.

Overview

Schools Today

The learning conditions in many U.S. schools are appalling. My former classroom on Chicago's West Side had no hand soap in the bathrooms, no access to a copy machine for teachers, and no books or paper or pencils in the classroom! Unbelievable! While teaching there, I made copies at my neighborhood office supply store. I personally purchased every piece of paper, pencil and crayon used in my classroom. Eventually, every book in the classroom was mine. Recess did not exist at this school because of the violence in the neighborhood; stray bullets could find us too easily on the playground. While this scenario may be remote from your child's school situation, it speaks to the lack of resources and the apathetic attitude towards some schools that exists in much of our society.

School administrators, teachers, and other staff have the best intentions. But they are being pushed to do more with less.

For instance, they are required to raise test scores despite less time, fewer personnel and more sparse resources. Also, they are required to teach more content while class sizes increase. Teachers must teach academic skills, organization, problem-solving, time management strategies and social skills with a 25:1 or 30:1 student-to-teacher ratio. While students do spend a majority of their waking hours in school, in-class instructional time often makes up roughly half of the school day. It is not practical to ask school teachers to teach a myriad of skills while also having to address the individual learning styles of every student.

Our system is flawed, and the changes needed to help teachers fulfill the almost impossible job that society demands will take significant resources. Ideally, parents and school personnel should work together to gain more time, money, and resources for elementary education. As mentioned, each child must have a solid base of skills to build on to succeed in school and in life.

Traditional "typical" schools and classrooms usually meet the needs of students who place in the average to above-average range in cognitive AND processing abilities. However, this leaves MANY children still struggling. Students at each end of the IQ range (roughly 40% of the population!), as well as children with processing difficulties, are less likely to have their learning needs met. Schools focus on efficiency because it is necessary. Anyone who does not "fit the mold" may be left behind. To truly customize the education of each child requires radical change, such as small student:teacher ratios (like, 10:1 or smaller), but radically positive change is not likely to come soon, in my opinion. As a professional educator, I would love for the public schools to have more time, personnel and support to help each child in every possible way.

As information is moving faster, the world is becoming more demanding. Schools are no exception. For many of our parents, for example, kindergarten was a place for structured play and socialization. Now, children acquire their first reading and math skills there. These skills need to be solid before they move into first grade, where the curriculum builds on that foundation. By third grade, students are "reading to learn" as opposed to learning to read. By nine years old, their reading decoding ("sounding out") and comprehension (understanding what they read) have to be pretty sophisticated. Because human development is uneven, many children are still working on solidifying these skills—but the curriculum moves on. This quick pace at such a vulnerable time of early growth can make the first few elementary school years troublesome for many children.

Standardized testing is another issue that society now demands. Low scores on standardized tests portray an unfairly negative picture of many children with diverse learning preferences and are therefore controversial. The wide-spread use of standardized testing for measuring students' abilities is unlikely to change soon. While I may not agree with it, its simplicity makes it a quick and easy way for schools to rate a learner.

The Picture of the Struggling Student

What characterizes a child who is truly challenged in school is subjective. Obviously, failing a subject counts, but these are the signs that he is challenged: he is often frustrated with school-related tasks, shows doubt in himself and constantly feels his performance is inferior to that of his peers. If he has trouble understanding, remembering and/or communicating information that has been taught repeatedly, he is struggling.

What about a child who is getting C's or even B's but has previously gotten A's? You will want to consider precisely why his grades have gotten lower. Being in a family where the parents are divorcing, moving into a new town and new school, or having a very sick brother or sister — these types of events can cause a child to focus less on school. Also, physical and mental development is uneven; many children have an easy year or two in school, then find a subsequent year more challenging. Later they often return to their initial level of success and confidence. Some students struggle with their schoolwork at first, then mature and become more competent. However, when grades continue to drop *in combination with* lower self-esteem, greater apathy and/or anxiety, then you and your child's teachers must explore this developing pattern.

What about a child who gets average grades but is a member of a high-achieving family with high expectations? Holding your child to high expectations can be positive, but it can blur into an emotionally unhealthy situation. Dr. Madeline Levine, psychologist, wrote a book about achievement, performance and effort called *The Price of Privilege*. She discusses our culture's current obsession with performance and accolades and criticizes the lack of value placed on effort and perseverance. When considering your children's school performance, you need to evaluate their effort and whether or not they ***are performing in a way that reflects their abilities***. If a child with average cognitive ability (scientifically speaking, with an IQ of around 100) is getting C's, then that child is performing consistently with his abilities. Our culture is obsessed with overachievement. Many of us often view "being average" and average performance (like getting C's) in a negative way. The grade of a C means "meeting expectations." Expectations vary greatly from one family to another and one community to another.

Children typically feel ashamed when they face difficulties in school. Parents may feel defensive, especially in front of other parents and school personnel. They may blame themselves, saying, "I feel so bad that he struggles with math the way I did! He gets that from me." They may also wonder aloud if a problem was caused by something they did or said in the child's very early years. In addition to the negative feelings of the parents, the children who struggle in school are almost always aware of their poor performance versus that of their peers. When children get the message, "You are not measuring up," they usually feel tremendous anxiety. Erik Erikson, a psychologist whose theory of human development remains influential, views child development as occurring in sequential stages. One of these stages he has named the 'Industry versus Inferiority' stage, typically beginning around age six. During this time, children get a sense of who they are based on how well they do in school and the quality of their work. They begin to see that performing well in school earns praise from the adults they love and respect, such as their parents and teachers. Children who fail to perform well may experience feelings of shame, which disrupt their growing understanding of themselves. If a child's growth during this stage is scarred, it negatively affects his long-term view of himself and growth in the later stages of development.

Unfortunately, negative feelings about school usually feed off themselves and grow over time.

Numerous studies show how stress negatively affects attention and memory in children and adults. Brain function changes under stress, negatively impacting memory and attention. Over time, this anxiety can turn into irrevocable apathy as a response from the student. John Medina, a developmental molecular biologist, wrote a book entitled *Brain Rules: 12 Principles of Surviving and Thriving at Work, Home* and *School.* He discusses at great length the impact of stress on learning and performance.

Negative labels can turn into self-fulfilling prophesies when the child begins to believe them, so it is best not to use them. Children, just like adults, like to feel successful, and they recognize that good performance is important to the people they love and respect.

Considering a child's desire to succeed, I remember a child I taught years ago. A second-grader — let's call her Anna, whose father labeled her "lazy." She was a precocious girl with long brown hair and glasses and had a sassy outlook on life. Anna and her mother were very close, coming into the school building together laughing and bubbly. Anna had attended a private school from preschool to age seven when I met her. Her schools' teaching philosophy was that the joyous journey of learning to read would be tainted by activities like phonics instruction. Such drills, the teachers felt, would turn learning to read into a boring activity, even a chore. Many children do learn to "crack the code" of print fairly independently through being read to regularly and following along on the printed page. They start to associate letters with the sounds they make by seeing adults read and model for them. Many children, however, do not learn best this way. Anna needed direct instruction with letters, the sounds they make, rhyming and the rules of words. Unfortunately, the school Anna attended was just not the right fit for her. She was not learning to read. Anna's father, however, thought it was a question of motivation. A doctor, he recalled that he had had difficulties in school as well. As we spoke, he remembered feeling like he had to work much harder than his classmates to get high grades. But he buckled down, worked hard, and got through school. In his view, he thought Anna should do the same. He saw himself in his daughter; in his experience, motivation solved the problem. Like Anna, school was probably harder for him. He may have had learning preferences that differed from the way he was being taught. His own learning needs likely went unaddressed by his teachers because he was intelligent, a hard worker, and conquered them himself.

Over time, Anna's father began to understand that his daughter was not lazy. She wanted to succeed but wasn't being taught in a way that was friendly to her brain. I was able to make changes with Anna's instruction, using a more a cognitive/clinical approach to learning, and she received additional tutoring outside of school. Within two years, she was reading at grade level.

When a child faces difficulties in school, resources exist to help him succeed; however, no quick fixes or shortcuts magically make the challenges go away. So far, we have not discovered how to change the fundamental way a particular brain works. A child who has difficulties with short-term memory, for example, will likely continue to have such difficulties, but he can learn strategies to help his memory. On top of that, he can use his other strengths to succeed. The concept of developmental readiness is also important. In Anna's case, she had weak auditory processing and auditory memory issues (very common among children who struggle with reading). Her brain did not efficiently store the sounds that corresponded with each letter. When shown the letter 'B', she needed a second or two to recall what sound B makes. While one or two seconds doesn't sound like much, it builds up when having to recall letter after letter while trying to read individual words, then sentences etc. Anthony probably had a similar issue, as well as poor working memory. He couldn't "hold" the first sound in his mind while working on the second, third, etc. sounds.

Developmental readiness varies from one child to another, and some students are open to learning a particular skill earlier than others. Our world moves quickly and we adults want things done in an efficient and linear way. Learning does not work that way. When working with children and their growth, we need to set aside the expectations we apply to other aspects of our lives and give our children time and support to develop a solid foundation of skills.

2

What Research Won't Tell You

I would not do justice to struggling students if I did not mention some of my own observations. As a classroom teacher, I was fortunate to spend many consecutive hours with students, allowing me to observe their behavior in many different situations, in large groups, small groups, 1:1, interacting with their peers at lunch and recess, etc. The amount of structure and nature of the interactions varied so much across these settings that I got to see students' strengths and weaknesses play out in different ways which helped me understand them in a well-rounded way.

One of the most important observations I have made while working with children with learning difficulties is that they often do not *notice* the details other learners do. For example, they may not notice that a multiplication chart is arranged with the smaller numbers toward the top, increasing from left to right and from top to bottom. Also, many students do not see the patterns in the structure of school.

They may not notice, for instance, that their history class is taught in chronological order, or that their daily and weekly schedules follow a pattern. For children who do not see patterns, everything is unpredictable and can catch them off-guard, making them anxious. An underlying reason behind anxiety is the unknown. Keeping this in mind helps us to understand how the structure of school and the tasks involved can leave children feeling tremendously anxious, even those who seem to be "normal" and "smart."

In addition, challenged learners often lack the "instinct" to use resources that have proven helpful. For example, if using a multiplication chart while working with multi-digit multiplication problems helps Joe, he still may not remember to use this resource unless reminded each time by a teacher. If remembering two assignments is difficult, he may not write down the assignments without being reminded. If remembering the key points of information from a paragraph is hard, he may not stop to summarize or take notes on what he has read without being taught this tactic.

Therefore, teaching children often involves teaching them *how* to best learn the material as well as *what* the actual content is. I have observed inflexibility in the way students cling to a strategy that isn't working. Rather than have the mental conversation, "Hmmm…this isn't working very well. Let me try another way," students who struggle in school often keep plugging away with the same inefficient approach. This frustrates them and leaves them feeling "stuck."

Most children do not want to stand out as "different" and will hesitate to use some resource (a number line, multiplication chart, etc.) that draws attention to themselves. They don't want other children to notice that they need extra help.

In addition, children who have learning difficulties often perform inconsistently. One day, they may totally "get it" and the next day, it's gone. It's as if they had never heard of the subject! This is a characteristic of a developing skill. Be patient. The skill will solidify with time and practice. Some skills may never be as solid as you would like; review them regularly and move on. I taught a student, Josh, who spent years trying to memorize multiplication problems. As of sixth grade, he still could not quickly remember these multiplication facts. So we moved on. When he needed to do multiplication, he used scratch paper to write out the problems since many facts did not pop out of his memory quickly. We learned that Josh needed extra time for certain math activities and we went with that.

If your child's teacher expresses concern about your child's progress in school but insists that you "wait it out" because he'll "mature into it," consider other alternatives. You may want to opt for private tutoring or other academic support programs (like Sylvan or Huntington Learning Centers). You may also decide to have the school test your child. A delay of months may occur between your request for an assessment and the testing, so start the process early. You can also seek a psycho-educational assessment outside the school. Some insurance and flex-spending plans cover part or all of the costs. Check with your insurance provider. Remember: you are more likely to regret inaction than action. So remain calm and get additional opinions.

3

Input: How Information Enters the Brain

The first step in evaluating the assignments your child has challenges with is to pick one task he finds difficult. Once you have selected that task, consider how the task starts. How is information being communicated to him? Is the teacher talking? Is she demonstrating how to solve a math problem? Is the child supposed to be getting the information from a chapter in his science book? The three basic ways to learn are: **auditory** (through hearing), **visual** (through seeing) and **haptic** (through touch). Input can come in more than one way and most schools request students to learn tasks by auditory and visual means.

- ## Auditory Input

Auditory input can be in the form of spoken language (verbal)
or sounds (nonverbal). For example, if a child listens to a
teacher give instructions, it is because he needs to use the
information she is sharing to correctly complete an upcoming
assignment: "Please finish reading Chapters 4 and 5 and
complete the questions at the end of Chapter 5." The input
here is auditory and verbal. An example of auditory nonverbal
information is the way, as a child, my mother whistled for
me to come in for dinner when I was playing outside. She
didn't use words, but the sounds she used carried the message,
"Come home now!" Another example is when someone is
talking and the children around him who want to hear the
teacher say, "Shhhhhhh!"

- ## Visual Input

Similarly, visual input falls into verbal and nonverbal
categories. Reading to get information is visual verbal input.
Looking at a picture, chart, graph or diagram and processing
what is shown is visual nonverbal input.

- ## Haptic Input

Of the three types of input, haptic is the least-commonly used
in the school setting. It too can be verbal—such as tactile
language systems like Braille—or nonverbal, such as feeling
the texture, weight or temperature of a surface or object.

Haptic learning takes place in physical education and art, two important but currently underappreciated school subjects. Both require competency in using objects and tools to achieve a goal or product. For instance, visualize a boy learning how to dribble a basketball down the court or shape clay into a small pot.

A pattern may reveal itself as you review the assignments that are hard for your child. For example, maybe he has more trouble when the information is auditory. James, a student of mine, could not remember auditory information. If I gave a set of three or four directions at once, he would get anxious and forget what to do. If I instructed, "Please read Chapter 7, then write answers to the questions at the end of the chapter," and, "When you finish, turn in your paper by placing it on my desk and then read your chapter book," James could not take in and remember that string of information. He was afraid to ask me what to do because I might think he hadn't been listening. James benefited from having the directions written on the board and summarized in bullet points. I would point to the directions on the board one at a time as I said them aloud. This gave James a place to look for a reminder when he completed one part of the instructions and was unsure of what to do next. Considering the type of input—auditory verbal—gave me an understanding of what was hard for James and how to work around it.

Response: How Information Goes Out of the Brain

4

After being taught specific information, students are usually asked to communicate their understanding. In the school setting, children may be directed to participate in a discussion, answer questions aloud or in writing, write a report or essay, or build a diagram or model.

• Recognition

Tests involving recognition have choices for answers that are provided in a list or word bank and the learner's task is to choose the correct one. Examples of tasks involving recognition include multiple-choice and matching activities.

- Yes/No

An example of an activity requiring this type of response is a true/false task.

- Same/Different

Activities requiring children to evaluate similarities and differences include the old favorite, "Which of these does not belong?"

- Body Movement/Gesture

Nodding your head yes or no, pointing to a picture, acting out an activity or giving a thumbs up in agreement are examples of gestures that communicate information.

- Manipulation

Manipulation involves using objects that already exist and moving them in a specific way. Moving blocks to recreate or continue a pattern, or putting together a jigsaw puzzle are examples of using manipulation to communicate understanding.

- Construction

Creating an object like a model, project, or sculpture are
examples of using construction to convey meaning.

- Visual Motor

Commonly seen in schools, this type of response requires
writing and/or drawing. Visual motor output can be verbal
(writing) or nonverbal (drawing).

- Auditory Motor

Auditory motor responses are needed every day when we are
required to speak for a majority of our interactions. Auditory
output can be verbal (speaking) or nonverbal (such as saying,
"Mmmm hmmm" in agreement.)

Brain Processes

Once the information is communicated to the student, it needs to be processed by his/her brain. Often, tasks require many coordinated brain functions to be done correctly.

Attention

The student has to pay attention, first and foremost. A child who is distracted internally (by his own thoughts, such as worrying about his sick mother) or externally (by an event going on around him, such as two boys seated next to him punching each other) will not process information very well. If focused, he can do better. It's as simple as that. You probably have heard the recommendation that you should sit front and center in a classroom if a lecture is being given. This placement helps prevent you from being distracted. I find it useful to think of attention in terms of filtering and focusing and impulse control.

Americans are bombarded by pieces of information all day, every day. Our attention abilities help filter out what is irrelevant to us at the time and what is important enough to make it to our conscious brains. From there, the selected information is processed by the brain and used right away or stored. Without our attention, we are overwhelmed with information—unable to sort through what is important and what is not in a timely manner. Focused attention protects us from drowning in worthless stimuli. Picking out the useful information that actually helps us understand something and accomplish a goal is a critical skill. School is one setting where lack of attention can lead to early failure for a child. A child who has problems with paying attention in school will likely have other academic problems. Instruction in practicing helpful strategies will probably benefit the student academically, socially and behaviorally. Healthy attention also keeps a student from spending too much time focused on something. This is called "perseverating." Attention needs to be flexible and cue a student to tell him to move on to other activities. For instance, if a child is upset about missing eight out of ten questions on a quiz given unexpectedly at the start of class, he may feel anxious about it for the rest of the class . . . or the rest of the day! He may not be ready to learn what is taught after that.

When I was a graduate student, we used a computer game to test a child's ability to pay attention. We used this activity as a type of screening. The game required the child to watch a computer screen that was blank at first. Every few seconds some letter of the alphabet would pop up for two seconds. The child was told to hit the space bar when the letter "B" appeared. Children who could maintain attention would do this with relative accuracy for several minutes.

The older the child, the longer the time they were expected to maintain focus, watching for the B and hitting the space bar accordingly. When we evaluated the data after this screening was completed, we looked at how many B's the child missed, and how far into the program (one minute? four minutes?) errors occurred. We also observed each child behind a one-way mirror, noticing if he lost focus during the task. Another measure was whether the child hit the space bar for other letters besides B — the ones he was supposed to ignore. If he tended to hit the space bar much more often than the B's appeared, that indicated impulsivity, a key challenge that diminishes attention. Explaining this screening activity illustrates how we study behavior in the quest to understand attention and how it affects performance in school.

What can distract a learner? Anything! Any visual or auditory input, such as a bug flying around the room or the hum of a fan, can distract some children. Tactile things can distract other children. For example, I had a student who could not wear corduroy because touching the ridges of the fabric would distract him throughout the school day. Some students are distracted internally by their own thoughts. For example, a child may think of something that reminds him of something else, leading his brain away from the input and into daydreaming.

Attention is responsible for how we take in and organize the important concepts as well as the small details we encounter. Attention also helps us slow down and think through the best way to tackle a problem so that we don't dive in and apply a rash, inappropriate strategy. Attention helps us sort through possible plans and select the best one based on our goals. We need to evaluate several options, find the one we think is best, and begin. Planning also requires a student to pay attention to his own thoughts and actions. Educators use the term "metacognition" to describe a student's awareness of his own thinking and learning. Paying attention not only to the information or tasks in school but to one's own tendencies and learning preferences leads to academic success.

• Impulse Control

Resisting impulses that throw us off track is important. This is called "impulse control," and the lack of it is an immense problem for many students. Inhibiting actions and initial reactions is extremely critical to academic success, especially when students are required to take standardized tests. Notice how test creators often include commonly-made mistakes in the answer options? For example, I once saw a test question like the one below.

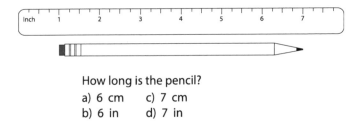

How long is the pencil?
a) 6 cm   c) 7 cm
b) 6 in   d) 7 in

Did you notice how the eraser-end of the pencil is not lined up with the edge of the ruler? A student who notices this will mentally adjust for it and calculate the pencil's length at six inches. But a student who has difficulty with impulse control may see the pencil tip at the seven-inch mark, quickly select that answer from the choices and move on. Impulse control has also been linked to anxiety, poor self-esteem and low frustration tolerance.

Children with attention problems may also be high stimulation seekers. Movement breaks can help some students with these types of challenges. Consulting with a pediatric occupational therapist (OT) who specializes in learning and attention is often helpful. An OT can prescribe the duration and frequency of a series of movement breaks appropriate for the child's age and needs. These breaks involve brief physical activities, such as a walk to the drinking fountain or stretches that use subtle movements a child can do in his seat. Another useful resource is the book *The Out of Sync Child* by Carol Stock Kranowitz.

These children are constantly looking for sensory input and find it nearly impossible to pay attention to anything that is not of high interest to them. Mentally setting aside a video game to play later and maintaining focus on getting homework finished first is nearly impossible for them. This is called an inability to "delay gratification." When I work with a child like this, I often say aloud, "What is important to us right now?" or "What should we pay attention to right now?" This helps the child tear his attention away from the snag in his sweater or the rip in the book cover and refocus on the task at hand.

Medication for children with ADHD has been in the media extensively in recent years. I am not a medical physician and my experience with using medication for children has been mixed. I have seen medication work very well for some students and terribly for others. This is an important choice to be evaluated by families based on the needs of their child. When considering medication, choosing a medical professional with experience in the field of ADHD is critical for a good outcome.

If you are concerned that your child has a problem with attention, consulting a clinical psychologist or other specialized health care professional may be useful. Information on the organization Children and Adults with Attention Deficit Hyperactivity Disorder, CHADD, can be found in the Appendix.

Perception

When discussing learning, perception is described as the process of using the necessary senses (hearing, vision, touch) to take in the information around you and make sense of it. Key in this process is figuring out which features are important and which are minor details.

- Discrimination: To take in information accurately, a learner needs to make distinctions among bits of information. For example, a child who is learning letters and their corresponding sounds needs to make the distinction between the letters M and N. While these letters look and sound somewhat alike, distinct features exist that need to be "noticed" by the learner's perception.

- Analysis and Synthesis: Understanding that whole units are often composed of parts, and the opposite of that—that parts can make wholes. To understand this, think of a child being shown a simple completed puzzle made up of five large pieces. Then the child is given the separate pieces and asked to reassemble them to make a complete puzzle himself. For the child to succeed, he must understand that the pieces in front of him can combine to form something bigger. It's the "seeing the forest for the trees" aspect of learning.

Memory

Like attention, memory is a big concept that greatly affects learning. Memory is often a problem for children who face challenges in school. Several aspects of memory exist, and they relate to each other. For example, a learner could very well have a strong memory for some events, such as going on a pony ride, and terrible memory problems with another, such as spelling words he needs to memorize for a spelling test. While you probably have a working knowledge of the concept of memory, let's expand it to better understand how the many aspects of memory influence your child's learning and school performance.

• Storing and Accessing

Memory is the ability to efficiently store and retrieve information. Efficiency refers to recalling information without much cognitive effort. If your memory is good, you remember without too much mental work or concentration. Retrieving information that is stored in your brain quickly and easily is called "automaticity." As a child moves through the grade levels, more and more information needs to be remembered automatically since other skills build on the basic ones. For example, automaticity of multiplication facts is necessary for a student when he begins solving complex math problems in algebra.

Problems arise when a child's brain does not have an efficient, organized storage system. Think of this storage system like a filing cabinet. When tax returns are in the same folder as the utility bills, it takes more time to find last year's tax return. If called on to answer a question in class, a student may not be able to pull the information to the forefront of his mind in time to answer his teacher. He will come across as someone who does not know the information, when he may just need more time to retrieve the answer. This frustrates the student and creates anxiety, making it even more difficult for him to pull up the needed information. When this happens repeatedly, the vicious cycle of disappointment and shame may begin.

When information is organized and grouped by shared traits or common themes, it is more likely to be remembered. This organization happens when a learner links incoming information with previously-learned information. For example, if a student is learning about the life cycle of a beetle, he may connect it to what he learned the year before about the life cycle of a caterpillar. Grouping similar information makes the input meaningful and more likely to be stored efficiently. Still, retrieving the correct information may be difficult to accomplish. If the information was not linked to other information, it may not have been filed in the brain very well. Or, maybe it was filed fairly well but never reviewed or revisited, and over time it was forgotten.

Graphic organizers are useful tools that help a child organize information better and improve his memory of it. Organizers help arrange concepts, procedural information or rote information. For instance, elements of fiction or sequential events can be shown in a graphic organizer to show the flow of a story plot. This organization makes sense and is more likely to be remembered by the student. Many types of graphic organizers are listed in the Appendix. You may not have had these tools when you were in school. Familiarize yourself with them so that you and your child can use them. (Children aren't the only ones who need to remember key information. You may find them useful yourself!)

Also, memory and attention work closely together, and it is often difficult to tease apart a problem with one aspect or the other as these two can be dependent on each other. Taking a hard look at what things a learner tends to remember well and what things he doesn't is an early step in problem-solving learning challenges.

• Auditory Memory

Filing and retrieving what we have heard requires auditory memory. In the early grades, children learn which sounds go with which letters. I went to graduate school with a student who had an exceptional auditory memory. He never took notes in class; he just sat and listened. He retained more of what we heard than those of us who took notes, recorded the lectures, and studied them later! Some brains just work that way. He was aware of his strong auditory memory and used it to his advantage. A poor auditory memory often manifests in decoding (sounding out words) problems, poor spelling and disorganization. Written instructions and/or visual references are often helpful tools for children with this challenge.

• Visual Memory

Visual memory is the ability to remember what was seen. Understandably, weakness in this area negatively affects decoding, reading comprehension, recalling demonstrations in class and correctly solving arithmetic problems. Providing additional auditory instructions, as well as practicing math work on grid paper, aids young learners.

Other Visual Processes

• Visual Sequencing

Visual sequencing describes the ability to perceive and reproduce numbers, letters and words accurately, as well as keep track of where you are looking. Using a separate answer sheet or copying from the board can be difficult for students with visual sequencing challenges.

Some children have problems with reading and math because they lose their place easily. They may also reverse or misread letters and numbers. Directions and instructions should be read aloud. Alternating colors when writing lists aid them in finding their place when they are looking back and forth. Color coding important notes is also helpful so the content really stands out visually and gets noticed.

• Visual Figure-ground

Visual figure-ground concerns the ability to see the important aspects of an image when the page is filled with other images and perhaps text as well. Too much visual data confuses the brain. Books can be overwhelming because of the many lines of print, and sometimes grammar and math worksheets are covered with designs and drawings. I suggest using a note card to keep track of the line being read and making worksheets clean and visually simple.

- ## Visual Discrimination

Visual discrimination describes the ability to process the difference between two objects. Does the student notice the important information—the differences? Keeping words and math problems well-spaced apart, with important visual information highlighted, such as the math operations signs, makes the content easier to grasp.

Spatial Processes

- ## Visual-Motor Integration

Visual-motor integration is similar to visual sequencing. When children have difficulty copying from a blackboard or a book and spacing problems when writing by hand on a page, it might be from a lack of visual-motor integration. Using a computer and voice recorder helps, as well as assessing the student's knowledge orally instead of grading his answers on a written test. Because the spaces are so clearly defined, using graph paper is a good tactic.

- ## Spatial Orientation

Spatial orientation relates to organization with space and time; the ability to keep track of materials and time, reading orally, writing by hand on a page, and tracking while reading.

Children who have a problem with spatial orientation often benefit from extra time to complete assignments. Another tactic is to break long assignments into smaller parts and have them address each part. You can assist them with organization by taking time to spot-check these students' homework binders and notes regularly, and using color-coding systems. Using week- and month-long calendars to show upcoming projects or events may also aid them in the planning process.

• Executive Functioning (EF)

Executive functioning is the sum of the processes the brain uses to set appropriate goals, then begin, maintain and complete the necessary steps to achieve them. Young children's goals include those that are academic, emotional and social. Disorganization and lost or late assignments signal problems with executive functioning (EF). When good time management is lacking, this points to an EF issue. Executive functioning also involves awareness and the monitoring of attention, self-control and behavioral flexibility. An ability to control impulses is critical, too, as an inability to do so will negatively affect the success of social interactions. Acting out by talking to other children and calling attention to oneself in other ways creates problems in school. Language, especially inner language (that voice inside your head that guides you in thinking and problem-solving) is involved, as is attention, memory and motivation. Development of EF skills continues throughout our lifespan as circumstances and expectations change. SO MANY children who face academic challenges have difficulty with one or more aspects of EF Because it is so complex and all-encompassing, additional resources are listed in the Appendix.

Processing Speed

This refers to the amount of time in which a learner's brain understands and organizes incoming information. Think of someone who responds quickly with a joke or retort in a social situation and you have identified a person who has this gift. Someone who needs to mull something over to mentally "digest" it is probably someone with a slower processing speed. In our fast-paced world, processing speed is often mistaken for a sign of overall intelligence. The truth is that although it is an observable aspect of intelligence, it does not accurately represent someone's total abilities. Fast processors tend to perform well academically, especially in an environment where fluency is emphasized. Another point: we need to be careful not to mistake fast processing speed for impulsivity. Impulsivity shows when a child quickly tosses off an answer without putting much thought into his response. A child who responds quickly yet inaccurately is probably acting impulsively.

Reasoning

The ability to solve problems is called reasoning. Inductive reasoning involves the ability to identify and apply rules. A child uses inductive reasoning when classifying, sorting and matching objects, as well as finding similarities and differences. The Woodcock-Johnson III Cognitive Abilities Assessment (currently the most widely-used IQ test) Concept Formation Subtest examines a child's inductive reasoning. The child is shown a set of colored shapes and must describe a rule that applies to those shapes. For example, when shown blue and red triangles, squares and circles, the student identifies whether they are blue or red. The rules get more complex as the test progresses.

Deductive reasoning involves the ability to draw conclusions from examples, like identifying an object based on its attributes. The simple game of "I Spy" uses deductive reasoning.

The Woodcock Johnson III Cognitive Abilities, Analysis-Synthesis Subtest measures the student's capacity to analyze visual puzzles and identify the missing part or parts.

Symbolization

When any person mentally represents something, he or she has symbolized it. In other words, an experience (an event that was seen, heard, and felt) is symbolized by a written design, noise, or bodily motion. When we hear someone talking, their language has meaning and conveys a message. If I say, "I fed the dog this morning." my spoken language has meaning. The words conjure up your understanding of the concept of a dog and my giving him food to eat. I haven't dragged you into my kitchen to show you the whole process of feeding the dog; that would be impractical and unnecessary.

Instead, I used language (symbols) to communicate that idea to you. The same is true when you read. The written symbols on the page have meaning and communicate a message. When we are the ones expressing ourselves, out loud or in writing, we are using symbols to convey a message. To best understand and use these symbols, whether they are heard, written or felt, we need to remember the symbol and what it represents.

Conceptualization

Forming a concept involves lumping a group of like experiences together. For instance, the word "zoo" may mean the local zoo to you as well as the ones visited in other cities. Riding in a "car" makes me think of my car, as well as other cars, and then vehicles in general (trucks, vans, etc.)

To conceptualize well, a child needs to be efficient at mentally organizing and storing this information in memory.

Intersensory Integration

This is the ability to integrate information from different sensory systems; putting what you see, hear, smell, taste and feel together to understand a total experience. In testing, for example, the teacher asks the student to point to the word that is said aloud when shown several word choices written on cards. He has to join what he hears to what he sees if he answers correctly. We may not often think about it, but we absorb the information around us through our senses. This information, translated into electrical signals, goes to separate parts of the brain. Once these signals have reached their destination, they unite with the other signals and recreate whatever was experienced as a whole. Past experiences, especially those that are similar, tend to influence how we integrate this sensory information and reconstruct an event. This explains why people who have experienced the same event often perceive it differently. Each person applies his own past experience to the translation made by his brain. Our senses are supposed to work together, but some are more over-powering than others. Hearing a song may bring up a certain memory, as well as certain smells may remind us of particular settings, people or experiences.

6

What It Takes to be Good at Reading

Debate continues regarding the range of skills needed to be a good reader. The key areas identified by the National Reading Panel in their 2000 report ("Teaching Children to Read")—the most recent—are my guides. They include phonemic awareness, phonics, fluency, vocabulary and comprehension. For detailed information about the National Reading Panel and their methods of evaluation go to: www.nationalreadingpanel.org

Phonemic Awareness describes the group of abilities needed to perceive and work with parts of spoken language, such as phonemes (individual sounds in words), syllables (groups of sounds), onsets (the beginnings of syllables), rimes (the middle and ends of a syllable) and complete words. Included in the overall concept of phonological awareness, phonemic awareness is focused on the awareness of and ability to manipulate individual sounds in words. Common activities in early childhood classrooms often incorporate rhyming and changing the first or last letters sounds in words to make new words, such as modifying "cat" to "bat." These activities help children learn that words are made of individual sounds and that these sounds can be broken into pieces or changed to make other words. Most of these skills can be developed before children are actually reading, using spoken word and rhyming games. A child with solid phonemic awareness can:

- isolate individual sounds in words ("What is the first sound in 'cat'?")

- delete sounds ("What is 'cat' without the /c/?")

- add sounds ("What word do you have if you add /s/ to the beginning of 'top'?")

- substitute sounds ("Here is the word 'hot.' What word do you get if you change the /t/ to /p/?")

- identify sounds ("What sound is the same in the words 'bat', 'bell' and 'bin'?")

- categorize sounds ("Which word does not belong in the group? 'Bat', 'bell', 'top', 'bin'?")

- blend sounds ("What word do you get with the sounds /c/ /a/ /t/?")

- segment sounds ("What different sounds do you hear in the word 'cat'? How many different sounds do you hear?")

Phonics is the link a person makes between the image of a letter (grapheme) and the sound(s) each makes. This essential basic reading skill is required for accurate spelling. We need to know what letter to write to represent each sound we hear to create words. While proven effective by teachers, reading specialists and parents or other caregivers, the direct teaching of letter-sound relationships is not always the way children are taught. If your child attends a school that emphasizes "whole language," it is likely that phonics has not been a focus. While the phonics-based versus whole language reading instruction debate rages on, it is true that some children discover the patterns on their own and others need more direct instruction regarding letter-sound correspondence.

Phonics-based instruction focuses on teaching letters and sounds separately in a large piece of content, such as a book. Whole-language approaches center on the meaning of the whole piece of text. The aim is to foster an appreciation for reading instead of using the often less-appealing skill 'n drill approach that phonics instruction primarily uses. Phonics once dominated reading instruction. After a time, whole language was viewed as the desirable, progressive way to teach reading. Now phonics-based instruction has returned. While the reading philosophy and approach varies from one school to another, as well as from one teacher to another, a balanced approach employing both occurs in many well-rounded early elementary classrooms. If you are not sure how your child is being taught to read, go ahead and ask his teacher.

Fluency describes the ability to read aloud smoothly and accurately. (Silent reading fluency is difficult to measure and so it usually is not.) The concept of fluency is not just about speed; fluent readers don't necessarily read fast. Instead, they read at a pace where they can still understand what they read and are expressive. They make reading aloud seem effortless. These readers have mastered phonics so well that decoding words is simple. This frees their cognitive abilities to focus on understanding what they read. Then they can use appropriate voice intonation and expression to demonstrate the meaning or the plot of the content. For example, using an angry voice to represent the giant in "Jack and the Beanstalk" shows an understanding of the story. Hearing adults read aloud allows young children to understand what fluency is.

Fluent readers recognize words quickly and easily. This "automaticity," a component of fluency, comes with practicing reading material that is easy-to-ever-so-slightly-challenging. Rereading the same material several times during the course of a few days also encourages automaticity and therefore fluency. Children may say, "But I read this story already!" Since they've read it, they know what it's about and feel they should be done with it. Good readers, however, practice reading the same text over and over, while striving to read it more smoothly each time. How easy or difficult should the reading material be? Easy text, known to educators as "independent level text," describes reading material that a child can read with 95% success. In other words, this text "trips up" the reader on approximately one word for every 20 words they read. The next level of difficulty is known as "instructional level text." This describes text that is slightly challenging to read for the student, but he can still comprehend what he is reading. Reading this text with a 90% success rate makes it instructional; the reader experiences difficulty with about one out of every ten words. Text that is too difficult for a reader, called "frustration level text," is so difficult for children that they cannot comprehend it. Decoding is slow, challenging, and inefficient. This describes any text which a child reads with less than 90% accuracy.

Many children really want to read more difficult text before they have the skills they need to make it accessible to them. The more public the book selection and reading processes are, the more competitive they may feel. This may lead to feeling social pressure to select more difficult books.

I encourage young readers to read the first page of a new book and keep track of words that stump them on the fingers of one hand. If they get to five words on the first page, the book may be too advanced for them at that time. Allowing children to try (and possibly not succeed) with reading books in private seems to work well. Difficult texts are often abandoned by the child's choice rather than by an adult telling them outright that the book is not suitable for them. Children don't want to struggle with reading. They want to enjoy the process. With support they will usually select appropriate books.

When you select reading materials for developing reading fluency, independent and instructional level text works best. These fluency passages should be fairly short. I suggest up to 200 words, maximum. Mixing it up by choosing text that includes fiction, nonfiction and poetry provides variety and opportunities for your child to explore various types of literature. This promotes growth in reading by broadening his knowledge of the choices of what he might enjoy reading in the future.

Fluent readers recognize words and comprehend them simultaneously. Young children, who are still developing phonemic skills, spend much of their energy on decoding words. Since this occupies much of their cognitive effort, comprehension suffers. They read at a slower pace and their reading sounds choppy as they pause to figure out words. They often make other types of mistakes as well, further disrupting their comprehension.

Specific knowledge of various word parts aids learning, too. A student familiar with affixes, which are little mini-words stuck to the beginning or end of words, can use this knowledge when he comes across unfamiliar words. Prefixes, found at the beginning of a root word, such as un-, re-, in-, dis- are common and easily understood as they have clear meanings. In the given examples, re- means 'again,' in-, dis- and un- mean 'not.' If you understand the verb "write," you can understand "rewrite" if you know the meaning of the prefix, 're.' Suffixes are word parts that go after the root word. For example, -ly can mean every (as in 'hourly'), like (as in 'cowardly') or it can turn an adjective into an adverb ('secondly'). Teaching these word pieces benefits your young student when he confronts new words. In addition, knowledge of root words is helpful. Understanding the meaning of the word 'migrate,' for instance, contributes to understanding other related terms such as immigration, migrant and migratory. Students who have studied some Latin are usually well-versed in the meaning and pronunciation of root words and affixes because many English words have Latin origins.

Comprehension: Understanding what we read is the whole point of reading! Reading is not a passive process. Good readers become engaged. They constantly think about and work to make sense of what they read. They have conversations in their mind with the text, asking questions, agreeing and disagreeing with characters' actions, making predictions and gathering information. These conversations vary depending on the purpose for reading. In reading an instruction manual, the reader seeks to understand how to use a device. When he reads a popular magazine, however, he may be looking for some advice, entertainment, or hobby tips. Readers use their existing knowledge to understand what they are reading. If the process is disrupted and they find themselves not understanding what they read, they use this awareness to try to solve the problem. Were there specific words or phrases they didn't understand? In that case, readers need to check for their meanings. Did they lose focus? If so, where? Then they should go back a few paragraphs and read the text again to get reoriented. Experienced readers have strategies for solving their own comprehension problems. These special skills and approaches take years of practice to develop. How can parents and teachers promote comprehension strategy development in their young students?

First, it's critical to teach students to monitor their own understanding while reading. This requires explicit instruction on how to notice when you get lost. This sounds obvious, but it can be difficult for many young readers, especially those who have already focused much of their cognitive effort in decoding words. Struggling young readers may finish a paragraph and have no idea of the meaning of what they just read! They concentrated so fully on grasping the words; they may not be able to identify the place in the passage where they stopped understanding. (In this case, the text may be too difficult. Find the appropriate instructional level text for your child so the decoding piece becomes automatic, freeing him to focus on making meaning.)

One useful learning activity requires an adult to read along silently with the student as he reads aloud. At the end of each paragraph, page or chapter (depending on the student's abilities), the child and adult summarize what is happening in that piece of text. I suggest that the student begin by discussing what he understands, and then identifying anything that isn't clear. This step-by-step approach prevents your child from blazing ahead when he does not understand what is going on. At the outset, summarizing can be difficult. Students may seize on less important but interesting details and completely miss the main ideas. You can model how to summarize "thinking out loud" about the main ideas. In this way, you guide the child's focus back to the big picture. You may also discuss any links between main ideas, another element usually missed by children when they initially learn to read.

Here is an example of how I modeled reading and summarizing with one of my first grade tutoring clients. We read a story about a mountain goat. The passage talked about his white coat and how it helped him blend into the snow, what animals were his friends, which animals he had to avoid because they may hunt him, and what food he ate. One day, he saw two hikers. He described them as "animals" because he had never seen people before. He observed that they walked on two legs, wore packs on their backs and made sounds to each other.

After we read, we had to pick one sentence out of three that best summarized the passage.

Me: 'Billy ate clover and grass from the mountainside.'

Erin: (student): I think that is a main idea.

Me: Hmmmm. Maybe. I'm wondering if it is a super big deal or just a little extra information. Let's see our other choices. 'Billy saw people for the first time.' That seemed like a big event when we read the story. What do you think?

Erin: I think that is a big deal. More than what he eats.

Me: I agree. But just to make sure, let's read the last choice. 'Billy liked the squirrels and the birds but stayed away from the cougars.' Hmmm...I'm wondering if that is a super big deal. Or maybe just a little extra information?

Erin: A little extra information. I think it's this one. (Points to the correct option, 'Billy saw people for the first time.')

An advantage of being with your child as he reads is that his difficulty with comprehension may be addressed right away. Sometimes the student's questions will be answered by continued reading. Other times the student needs to stop reading to discover the meaning of an unfamiliar word or discuss an unknown phrase. The job of the adult is to model the internal thinking that practiced long-time readers have inside their minds while reading. For example, I was reading another book with Erin and a character in that book said, "Well, I'll be a monkey's uncle!" She never heard this expression before. The oddness of the statement derailed her thinking. She didn't understand what she read for the rest of the page! When we paused our reading to discuss the passage, she shared that her comprehension "red flag" went up when she came to that line. We discussed what it meant, went back and reread that piece and the rest of the page, and then she understood. I praised her for her awareness that something had been "off" in her understanding. A few pages later, a character did something that was inexplicable at that point in the story. Erin expressed her confusion and thought that maybe if she went back and reread part of the chapter, she would understand the character's action. Serving as a model for thinking, I said, "Maybe if we keep reading, we will get more information about why this happened." I guided her away from the intention of rereading. I knew that the information needed to fully understand the text still lay ahead. Students are not always efficient at using strategies while they learn, so some guidance from an adult is valuable. (Of course, this also may require the adult to do some preparation and be familiar with the text!) What should you do if your child is adamant about going back and rereading? I say let him, even if you know it will not solve the problem.

Students need to experiment with problem-solving. This is how they learn what is useful in different situations. If your child feels strongly that he knows how to solve a reading problem, let him try. In this situation, the biggest accomplishment was that the student became aware of the interruption in his understanding and then wanted to take action to repair it.

As the reading mentor, attempt to find the balance between allowing the child to experiment but do not waste too much time on fruitless action. Achieving balance varies with each learner. When you and a child get into a stand-off, this interrupts learning. My rule is that after five minutes of pointless looking/rereading, we carry on together to discover if the answer is just ahead.

Flexibility, when a reader uses comprehension strategies, is essential. While reading, you may start using one strategy, recognize that it is not working, and leave it behind to try another one. Young children and others who feel insecure in their abilities, however, are more likely to stand their ground. They may repeat the same strategy time after time. Gentle encouragement from you, coupled with the child's developing confidence in his reading competence, soon enables a young learner to be less defensive and open to various approaches. I coach parents and teachers alike to be exceedingly patient in this process. Nothing I can say or do makes it any easier;

it is hard. Eventually, with time and practice, the necessary breakthroughs occur.

When you stop reading to discuss and clarify, the reading mentor may ask questions to guide the new reader toward linking what he read to his existing knowledge. The mentor may also identify the most important information, the order of events, or any other key element from the text. As the student advances in comprehension, he may choose to ask the questions instead. Alternatively, the two may just discuss and summarize the text. Eventually, the adult will not be needed in the same way. The purpose of the adult in the team is to model the active thoughts of a competent reader, voice questions and emphasize important information. Ideally, over time, the competent reader role becomes internalized by the student. The new reader's own brain will ask similar questions to those that the adult reading mentor used and said out loud. To achieve this goal takes years of practice.

Another helpful tool, the graphic organizer, can be a chart, web, diagram or any other visual tool that organizes information. Graphic organizers make concepts, relationships and information visually clear. One example is representing simple statistics in a pie chart. The text reads, "An adult's 24-hour day may be easily divided into three parts: eight hours for sleeping, eight hours for working, and eight hours for family, friends and recreation." Right now, you can easily create a mental picture of a circle (pie) divided into three parts (slices). This simple chart helps the brain create more meaning out of the words. When you read a story with a first grade student, a graphic organizer can help by identifying the beginning, middle, and end of it. When a middle school student studies the classes of species, a hierarchical web is appropriate. (See the Appendix for some helpful graphic organizers.)

To select an appropriate graphic organizer for a specific purpose, you need knowledge of text structure. Initially, students can be offered one or two organizers for text that is fiction and one or two for nonfiction texts. At first, the teacher/adult should select the best graphic organizer for young readers. As your young students become more familiar with the structure and purpose of different graphic organizers, they can begin selecting their own with your guidance.

Explicit instruction about text structure aids readers in understanding what they read. It also sets expectations about what kind of information they should expect to see as they continue reading. A fiction story presents differently than a poem does. While adults have already learned this, young children are surprised and interested in it. Children can learn about setting, characters and plot in fiction. In later grades, when students begin reading nonfiction, such as science textbooks, lessons in how textbooks and their different parts, chapters, and sections are organized prove useful.

When reading text with new vocabulary and unfamiliar terms, searching for and using context clues leads the student toward the meaning of text as well. The clues to a word's meaning are often given in surrounding words, phrases and sentences. Following is a short list of some of these types of clues. They include definitions, restatements, examples and descriptions.

- The birds are **migratory**, moving from one location to another as the seasons change.

- Sarah was in a **melancholy** and gloomy mood.

- Joseph jumped for joy to show his **enthusiasm**.

- Mr. Jones was so **baffled** that he scratched his head and tried to make sense of what he had just seen.

While context clues are not necessarily hard to find, students usually need to be taught strategies for finding and using context clues appropriately. Eager to make sense of what they read, children sometimes think there is a clue when no helpful information exists. For example, a sentence that reads, "The pilgrims lived a **pious** lifestyle," does not give any useful information to a reader who does not know the meaning of the word "pious." Compare that sentence to the following sentence that contains context clues: "Because of his religious beliefs, he lived a pious lifestyle, giving money to poor people and praying many times each day." Explicit instruction on how to identify context clues as a comprehension strategy takes time. Young children enjoy cracking the code of a mysterious word for themselves and gaining competence—just like adults.

Spelling: Spelling exercises appear regularly in the curriculum of the early elementary years. Teachers often give spelling tests in which they pronounce words from a list out loud and the students spell them. (Could this be one of the only practices that hasn't changed that much since we adults did it?) Teachers also regularly assign and grade writing projects such as stories, essays, and reports. A child may be stronger in one area of spelling and not in another. Often, memorizing words in isolation for the weekly spelling test (especially if these words fit a certain pattern or theme) is easier than spelling those same words accurately while writing a story. Writing tends to be extremely difficult for many young students, because it involves so much mental energy, memory, and coordination of effort. Think about what's required. You have to form thoughts, hold them in your head and record them (whether through handwriting or typing) in a way that makes sense. Many adults struggle, too, when attempting this!

Evolving into a strong speller is closely tied into understanding phonics, which includes having keen phonemic awareness. Practice with phonics usually serves as a partial remedy for spelling difficulties. Since a lack of consensus exists among education researchers about spelling development, I'll summarize what I've learned from the various experts.

Children start spelling by writing scribbles that mimic what they see adults write. At first, the scribbles will be meaningless if you try to read them. Often a child will tell you what he intends them to mean if you ask. He'll say something like: "Look! I made a list of what I want from Santa Claus! This first thing is ____. The next is ____." These scribbles will progress into containing a handful of letters that he has learned. Over time, the scribbles become strings of letters, which may or may not stand for the sounds those letters represent. As children grow in their knowledge of phonics, they begin to represent some of the sounds they hear in words with the right letters. Usually the first letter of a word is also the first letter to be written accurately. For example, sister may be written as "stxc" or something similar, with an accurate letter being the one that represents the first sound. Then the ending and middle sounds start to be represented more accurately. Sister may become "sstr" or even "sitr." Consonant blends (such as cl, br, st), consonant digraphs (such as ph, th, sh) and vowel sounds still tend to be inaccurate, but most sounds will be represented. Time, growth and experience with words aids a child in understanding how word patterns work, for example, that the letters "ph" when found together, make a sound like /f/. This increasing knowledge is reflected in the child's spelling as he increasingly writes the correct representations of these sounds.

Developing spellers overgeneralize rules, making mistakes like writing any word that ends in the long /e/ sound using a "y." Words like "tree," "marquee," and "ski," for instance, contain that sound but do not follow that rule. Again, time and experience will allow your child to grow into mastering more spelling rules and patterns. He learns odd words because they catch his attention while he's reading. He creates his own strategies for reading, spelling and remembering different words if his phonemic awareness, attention, perception and memory work together.

With so many elements playing a part in spelling mastery, it is no wonder so many children struggle with spelling. Some children need explicit phonics instruction to conquer the reading challenges they have. As mentioned, this helps with spelling.

Each of us knows at least one person who is still a poor speller as an adult. I have a friend who is gifted in science and math. However, her poor spelling shocks me! With so many accessible resources available, the most obvious being spell-check, few excuses are now acceptable for poor spelling. I encourage children to use spell-check when they write pieces that run longer than a list of spelling words or a paragraph. I coach them to use spell-check as the last step before considering a written assignment complete and turning it in.

As those of you who use spell-check know, it does not solve all spelling problems. You want to coach your child in how to approximate words well enough to make the real word appear as one of the choices that shows in spell-check. Recognizing the presence (or absence) of the targeted word in a list of word choices is a useful and practical skill. Students need to be able to *recognize* correct spellings. This is different, yet related to generating accurate spellings.

Although students should strive to recognize reading and writing word patterns, when a child is capturing ideas on paper, I would rather have him devote his energy to communicating his ideas. I encourage my students to work on their first drafts of written assignments without paying too much attention to spelling words correctly. "We'll fix it later," I tell them.

Of course, students must be able to spell the words they use well enough to remember what they meant! This is where phonics skills reveal themselves. If two children are writing stories about their sisters, the child who writes sister as "suzter" will probably have an easier time rereading, making sense of, and improving his writing than the one who records sister as "ztr." So, from a practical perspective, a solid base of phonics knowledge is needed just to begin to write. Until a student possesses this knowledge, he can use an adult's help capturing his ideas. A teacher or mentor may take dictation or record the child's talking voice as he tells his ideas. Then they can work together to write it later.

As a teacher and tutor I've noticed many children dislike writing any word if they are not 100% sure it is spelled correctly. Some students would rather have a completely blank page than write a sentence with some misspellings. Adults need to encourage and not criticize early spelling attempts. Your child won't learn how to spell if he doesn't take the opportunity to make mistakes! Sometimes, the child can't bear not being correct. As a reading mentor, this is the opportunity to remind him that we all make mistakes—especially when we're learning something new.

Use proven strategies when aiding your child to study spelling words. Usually, spelling units contain words that fit a certain pattern, from "a-with-a-silent-e" to words with the pattern "–ough." Explicit instruction and related practice with the sounds made by certain letter combinations is helpful. Phonics programs like The Wilson Method and Lindamood-Bell

Learning Processes effectively address the letter patterns that make certain sounds. We may tell children that the "e" at the end of the word does not make any sound, but it does "boss the a" to say its own name in a word such as 'rake.' With simple and memorable explanations like this one, students may recall specific rules and remember them better.

When we talk about spelling, we talk about accurate ("right") spelling and appropriate spelling. Accurate means the word is spelled correctly. Appropriate spelling refers to a word that is spelled incorrectly, but the sounds are marked and we can see the reasoning behind the speller's mistakes. For example, a child who spells dolphin as "dolfin" has spelled the word appropriately but inaccurately. We can understand why he would spell dolphin this way…because it does indeed sound like an /f/ in the middle. This is an example of a speller who has a solid understanding of phonics but just hasn't yet had the experience to put "ph says /f/" in his memory. His strong attempt at an accurate spelling of the word deserves some credit and praise.

7

What It Takes
to be Good
at Math

arly Counting Abilities: Young children need to have a solid understanding of the one-to-one correspondence in counting by kindergarten. Many children struggle with this; they assign two numbers to one object or skip an object—especially if they are trying to count quickly. Slow accurate counting means a young child should say just one number for every object he touches or moves while counting. Also, the numbers said aloud while counting should be in the correct order, with the last number representing the quantity of objects. Young children grow in their ability to understand that the objects being counted can be counted in any order and the total quantity remains the same. (For example, counting ten blocks lined up left-to-right proves to be the same amount as those same ten blocks counted right-to-left.) These basic counting principles serve as the foundation for a child's early math development.

The first number facts taught to most young children are related to addition and draw on the ability to count objects or quantities and continue counting. In class, I say, "count on" to include more. The "counting on" process is used by a learner when he starts with one addend and continues counting from there to add the second. For example, if the learner is faced with the problem 8 + 2, he may say "Eight" aloud, then "Nine, Ten" to show the addition of the second addend, the 2. He may or may not use his fingers to show the counting on, and he may start with the 8 or the 2, although starting with the 8 is a more efficient, mature approach. Young children usually do not start using the counting-on strategy until they have gained experience with addition. Do not be alarmed if your first grader does not use this approach. He must clearly show that he understands the concepts of counting and adding. Similarly, the "counting down" process is used for subtraction.

Facts: Your child needs to master basic addition, subtraction, multiplication and division math facts, as well as rules and procedures, to succeed in math. In the later elementary grades and onward, more complex problems build upon your child's grasp of these basic facts. The more readily a young student can recall the needed math information, the more mental energy he has to tackle the complexities of the problem. He doesn't have to get bogged down by the underlying computation. For example, a student is given a problem to find the area of a triangle with the base being 4 and the height being 8. He must use the formula, 1/2 base times height, to calculate the area of a triangle. If dividing the base, 4, by 2, has not been mastered, the student is more likely to get the problem wrong than if he can quickly remember 4 divided by 2 equals 2.

Along with mastery of these basic facts, students need to be able to write numbers clearly and accurately. They must also know what the signs mean from a conceptual standpoint. For instance, the minus sign signifies subtraction, which means taking away and making smaller. Last, they need to understand the quantity the number represents (have "number sense"). While it seems obvious to most of us that 10 is larger than 8, young children with poor number sense may not readily understand it. Number sense refers to that concept of a number line that we visualize in our minds. We know that numbers get larger as we move right on the number line and they get smaller as we move left. If we move right two spaces, we are counting up by two's. We also understand that 10 spaces to the right and 10 spaces to the left are the same distance from zero, but one number is positive and one is negative.

This is not common knowledge for many children who struggle with math, especially students with visual perception challenges. The concepts of space, distance from one number to another, and the direction of right and left on the number line do not mean much to these children. Many of these learners also struggle with the concept that 10 represents ten of something, and 12 represents two more. Young learners need to be taught explicitly and early about the number line, number patterns, and quantity—ideally in kindergarten and first grade. Even children with solid visual perceptual abilities struggle with these concepts. Their attention, perception, reasoning, memory and conceptual abilities are occupied with learning, remembering and accessing the basic math facts. Any glitch in one or more of these aspects of learning can disrupt the child's understanding and performance in math.

Continued practice with facts should be a focus. If a child does not understand the concept after teaching it one way, try another. For example, one of my students was struggling with rounding. We began with rounding numbers to the nearest 10. I used a tool—a tape measure—as my number line, and extended the tape measure across the table. Together, we identified all the 10s on the number line (10, 20, 30 and so on) and marked them with arrow post-it notes. We looked at the first problem in her homework assignment: 26. I asked her to find 26 on the number line. I then asked "What two tens is it between?" She answered the 20 and the 30. I asked which it was closer to, the 20 or the 30? Together, we counted that 26 was 6 "hops" away from 20 but only four "hops" away from 30. She recognized that 26 was closer to 30. I could tell that she understood the concept and procedures when the number line (tape measure) was in front of her. When we tried to solve similar problems without the tape measure, however, she was stumped again. At that point in her lesson, I decided to teach her another way to solve the problem.

I began by writing the following rule on a notecard:

1, 2, 3, 4 LEAVE ME ALONE!

5, 6, 7, 8, 9 Round up!

Then, I told her that if you are being asked to round to the tens place, underline that place. (For instance, the number 26 looks like 2̲6.) Now circle the "neighbor" to the right, which is the 6. "Is 6 in the 'Leave me alone!' group, or in the 'Round up!' group?" I asked her. She decided to round up, and the 2 (for 20) rounded up to 3 (for 30), and the 6, which had been circled, changed to a 0. (This is easy for the student to remember because the circle makes it look like a zero.)

I don't like this method as much. For me, the number line method makes more sense. I can picture the number line in my head when I think about rounding. But this student liked the second method in which you underline the desired rounding place, circle the neighboring number to the right and then apply the rule. I noticed she continued to use it after our lesson. Flexibility in your approach to teaching is key when working with individual students. Each of us learns somewhat differently.

Another important aspect of being able to accurately solve the number fact aspect of a problem has to do with number formation and spacing. The act of writing numbers legibly, spaced well and in the correct order can be burdensome to a young student. Several opportunities for errors exist when he attempts to copy from a board or text book. This copying slows the problem-solving process and uses valuable mental energy. Something as simple as not lining up numbers in the correct column may contribute to an incorrect answer. Many bright, capable students struggle with the actual writing and spacing aspects of solving problems, especially in the early- and mid-elementary grades. Getting to the one right answer—which is typically the graded result—is the goal, not the steps leading to it.

Children with visual perceptual and visual sequencing challenges often struggle with the spacing of problems on a page. Reducing the amount of copying from a board, overhead or book helps these students. Another aid, graph paper, helps such students line up problems correctly. Using highlighters or small post-it notes to color-code different aspects of the problem, such as place value and operation signs, offers them visual clues about what to do.

Making Sense of Math Concepts: Students may have trouble applying math concepts to their everyday lives. This application is one test of whether they truly understand the concepts. While many aspects of math can be memorized, the information will not be as meaningful or remembered as well if it is not connected to tangible objects. For example, your child may memorize the fact that 1/3 is less than ½. If he can clearly visualize two identical cookies, one cut into thirds and one being cut in half, he is likely to remember which is smaller and which is bigger. If he gets the third, he will get less of his cookie! That's memorable! Relying on rote memory only, instead of a meaningful connection, can negatively affect a student's success in math. Incorporating math into daily activities, such as counting change and measuring ingredients is helpful.

Students who struggle with math reasoning may have difficulty figuring out the best procedure to use to solve a particular problem. Typically, they also fail to remember similar problems they have been given and solved. If they did remember, they would recall and use some of the same steps in their approach to the new problem. Extra practice in math problem-solving takes some of the pressure away as the child conquers problem after problem and grows in confidence.

Language: Math has its own language and vocabulary. Children with language difficulties struggle with the terminology in mathematics just as they do with terminology in other subjects. The context for math terms should be taught, with students taking notes and completing activities that work from more structure or "hints" (fill-in-the-blank sentences using the term and its definition) to less structure (the student writes his own sentence that defines the word), an approach mentioned earlier to build a basic vocabulary for reading. Begin teaching the basics—terms such as greater than, less than, equal to, and equation.

Word problems strike fear into most young students, but especially those who can't understand what they are being asked! One common trouble area is word problems that compare two amounts: Joy had 17 lollipops and Sam has 23. How many more does Sam have? Children with language difficulties typically get thrown off by the presence of the word "more" and attempt to solve this problem by adding when it requires subtracting.

Visual/Spatial and Perceptual Problems: Some students cannot easily visualize math concepts. Remember the number line we mentally picture to track where numbers or quantities are in relation to each other? Imagine having no reference points for these concepts! Reading graphs or thinking and comparing the sizes of real life objects that have to be imagined is nearly impossible for some students. Being able to mentally picture what a shape will look like if it is flipped or rotated may also escape them. Most of us take these abilities for granted. (We shouldn't!) Students with visual and spatial perceptual challenges have to rely on memorization to solve problems. This mentally fatigues them and then they are more likely to lose attention. Also, textbooks and worksheets that include a lot of writing and designs can be visually overwhelming. To make it easier for these students, fewer problems should be placed on a page with few additional designs and enough blank space to show how the problem was solved.

Like other academic areas, math uses the mental processes of attention, perception, and memory. Some students forget what they are doing while in the middle of attempting to solve a problem. Some have trouble following a procedure step-by-step or remembering each step necessary to solve a problem. (To address this, keep a page listing the steps for them to serve as a reference when they need it. Also, expect to remind students that they have these reference sheets to rely on.) Picking out the relevant information in a word problem takes skill. Many of them include a piece of irrelevant information inserted to try to trick the student. The student has to use his reasoning ability to determine what information is important and what is not. When he has completed the problem, he needs to evaluate whether or not his solution makes sense. Complex problems often ask the learner to mentally switch from one task to a different one to solve another part of the problem and this can cause confusion.

Working memory problems often present themselves when children show slow counting speed and have difficulty keeping numbers in their working memory while counting. (For these children, the "counting on" procedure doesn't usually work because they can't often hold the first addend in their minds while counting on for the second addend.) Long-term memory issues are revealed when children experience difficulty retrieving facts and concepts from memory.

Conclusion

What Now?

We expect children to ask questions when they don't understand something clearly, even though children often do not even know where to start with their questioning. They may be so confused that they don't know what to ask, so you need to try different approaches. Also, a student may feel embarrassed to ask for help, especially when he fears he is the only one who doesn't understand some piece of material. In my experience, sometimes students do well in math class and yet perform poorly on tests. This may result because tests, especially standardized tests, jump from one concept to another with each different problem. The mental gymnastics involved in solving these problems accurately can be both challenging and mentally exhausting for young learners. So, after listing the many possible problems children may encounter in math, we need some helpful strategies and special tools for children that experience difficulty in language and math areas of school, as well as for children who struggle to stay organized in general.

While most schools will make accommodations for individual children, some will have to be convinced of the need. With encouragement, some children readily use additional materials or strategies to help themselves. A few are hesitant and do not want to stand out as being different. If you can find out why a child is struggling, you are better able to figure out specifically how to help. Please use the Appendix for more information and ideas.

Appendix

Strategies for Teachers and Parents of Students Struggling in School

- Evaluate input, processes used and responses. Use this framework to identify and evaluate mistakes.

- Constantly ask yourself, "What exactly does this child find difficult?"

- Give directions one step at a time.

- Give directions in writing and aloud.

- Use an explicit, structured phonics program like the Wilson Reading System, Lindamood-Bell Learning Processes or similar for children struggling with decoding skills.

- Preview books before reading them with your child. Discuss the topic, themes and helpful background information. Use the information on the back cover, illustrations and reviews for preview material.

- Have your child read with a reading mentor/ partner (adult, older student).

- Make predictions about text before reading.

- Link new information with old by discussing what was just learned with information learned previously.

- Think and "wonder" aloud to summarize, and ask and generate questions after reading with your student.

- Use a marker, such as a note card, to help the young reader track his reading.

- Break down words into meaningful parts such as prefixes, suffixes, and root words.

- Have number lines, multiplication charts and other visual aids available.

- Use manipulatives in math, such as objects for counting, a number line, ones/tens/hundreds blocks, rulers, measuring cups etc. Anything that can make a seemingly-abstract math problem more real-life related helps children learn and solve problems.

- Think about ways to address a particular problem and speak the steps aloud while solving it. (This is another example of "thinking aloud" as you solve a problem. You are modeling your process, not just the answer.)

- Share what you find useful with your child, such as a Franklin speller, children's dictionary, reading pen or spell-check.

- Use math in everyday situations, such as telling time and paying for purchases.

- If possible, seat a distractible child away from distractions (the doorway, a window, a distracting student) and closer to the teacher.

- Offer extended time for assignments when appropriate.

- Create graphic organizers for improving reading comprehension.

- Advise your child to complete homework assignments in this order: easiest, hardest, and all others.

- Make certain your child has a homework environment that is clean, stocked with supplies, and as free from distractions, such as TV noise and other people talking, as possible.

- Your child should be guided to study in the same place every day.

- For best results, homework assignments should be started within 30 minutes after your child arrives home from school.

- Some students need to give themselves 2-minute or 3-minute movement breaks to steady their attention and energy levels.

- Teach and use subvocal rehearsal (whispering quietly) to hold information in short-term memory temporarily.

- Periodically stop reading to discuss important concepts.

- Use maps, charts and graphic organizers to organize ideas and concepts.

- Highlight important information, such as vocabulary terms and events in a story.

- Review previously-learned material regularly.

- Use a number line for math procedures to solidify understanding of addition, subtraction, multiplication and division.

- Coach your child to use graph paper when he's solving math problems. This assists with both neatness and accuracy.

- Use a calendar to keep track of assignments and due dates.

- Worksheets should be visually clean and free of unnecessary designs, drawings, or graphics.

- Write down all steps required to solve a problem; no "mental math."

- Avoid asking your child to copy from the board; print information or directions.

- Write notes before instruction that require the students to fill in words and phrases as they are given in the lesson. (As most of the notes are already recorded, the student listens and writes in answers as he hears them given in the lesson.) Teachers call this "cloze" activities.

- Post lists of materials and procedures so that students can refer to them as needed.

- Use color-coding in various ways to make organization of school materials easier. For instance, color-code folders by subject area: yellow for reading, blue for math.

- When creating learning material on a computer, use a font like Comic Sans. The 'a' in this font is more reader-friendly than in other fonts that use 'a'.

Resources for Teachers and Parents

Helpful Books

Overcoming Dyslexia: A New and Complete Science-Based Program for Reading Problems at Any Level by Sally Shaywitz, M.D.

The Whole-Brain Child: 12 Revolutionary Strategies to Nurture Your Child's Developing Mind by Daniel J. Siegel, M.D. and Tina Payne Bryson, Ph.D.

NurtureShock: New Thinking About Children by Po Bronson

Why Don't Students Like School: A Cognitive Scientist Answers Questions About How the Mind Works and What It Means for the Classroom by Daniel T. Willingham

When Can You Trust the Experts: How to Tell Good Science from Bad in Education by Daniel T. Willingham

Brain Rules: 12 Principles for Surviving and Thriving at Work, Home and School by John Medina

The Art of Teaching Reading by Lucy Calkins

Teaching Essentials: Expecting The Most and Getting The Best From Every Learner, K-8, by Regie Routman

Visualizing and Verbalizing: For Language Comprehension and Thinking by Nanci Bell

The Reading Teacher's Book of Lists by Edward B. Fry, Ph.D. et al.

The Math Teacher's Book of Lists: Grades 5-12 by Judith A. Muschla and Gary Robert Muschla

The Price of Privilege: How Parental Pressure and Material Advantage Are Creating a Generation of Disconnected and Unhappy Kids by Madeline Levine

The Overachievers: The Secret Lives of Driven Kids by Alexandra Robbins

Speech to Print: Language Essentials for Teachers
by Louisa Moats, Ph.D.

Wilson Reading System by Barbara A. Wilson

The Out-Of-Sync Child, by Carol Stock Kranowitz

Testing for Kindergarten: Simple Strategies To Help Your Child Ace The Tests For: Public Schools Placement, Private School Admissions, Gifted Program Qualifications by Karen Quinn.

What Your First Grader Needs To Know: Fundamentals of a Good First-Grade Education by E.D. Hirsch, Jr. This whole series, available for most grade levels, is a helpful guide to common curriculum by grade.

A Board Game Education: Building Skills For Academic Success, by Jeffrey P. Hinebaugh

Websites

Educators Publishing Service (www.epsbooks.com)

www.ldonline.org
Includes downloadable documents, updates in the field of learning disabilities, information for parents, teachers, and specialists.

www.wrightslaw.com
Information about special education law, including updates, frequently asked questions (FAQs), and law interpretation.

www.yellowpagesforchildren.com
Start here and then search for local resources by state.

www.pldonline.org
Content for professionals who specialize in learning disabilities and a good resource for parents and teachers.

Glossary of Reading Terms

Phoneme: the smallest part of spoken language; an individual sound. English has about 41 phonemes, although these differ slightly, depending on a speaker's regional accent. Each phoneme is usually represented by one or two letters. For example, the word "cat" has three phonemes /c/ /a/ /t/, and so does the word "chop" because the *ch* work together to form one sound, /ch/ /o/ /p/. The word "oh" has just one phoneme.

Phonics: the understanding of the relationship between the sounds (phonemes) in language and their graphemes, or letters that symbolize these sounds in written language.

Grapheme: the smallest part of written language. Graphemes are the symbols (letters, combinations of letters) that represent the sounds we hear in spoken language.

Phonemic awareness: the ability to hear, identify and manipulate phonemes (sounds) in words

Syllable: a word part that must contain a vowel

Onset: the initial consonant sound of a syllable, like the /c/ sound in "cat" or /th/ in "think"

Rime: the part of the syllable that contains the vowel sound and anything that follows, such as /at/ in "cat" or /ink/ in "think"

Morpheme: the smallest part of a word that has meaning. This includes prefixes, and plural "s"

Morphology: the study of the construction of words

Orthography: the study of correct spelling

Consonant Blends: combinations of two or three letters at the beginning or end of a word, with each letter keeping its sound: bl, cl, fl, gl, pl, sl, br, cr, dr, fr, gr, pr, tr, sp, sw, sc, sk, st, sm, sn, tw, scr, spr, spl, str, mp, nd, nk, ng

Consonant Digraphs: two letters combine to make one sound: ch, th, wh, sh, ph, ng, ck

Vowel Blend: two vowels are next to each other in a syllable, the first one usually makes the long sound while the second one stays silent: ea, ai, ie, oa, ay, oe

Dipthong: two vowels connected to make one sound: ou, ow, igh, oi, oo, ee

R-controlled vowel: When a vowel is next to a r, it changes the sound the vowel makes: ar, er, ir, or, ur

Sight words: Words that readers need to memorize and know just by seeing them because they do not follow regular phonological rules or patterns. Many of the most common words in English are sight words, such as *they*, *of* and *the*.

Nonsense words: These are words that do not exist in contextual language but are made using existing phonics patterns, such as scrill or scritch. The purpose of asking children to read these words is to get a look at the child's phonics knowledge and skills. Many children who struggle with phonics cleverly memorize many words by sight, and reading with a child who does this may give an inaccurate picture of the child's abilities. Asking a child to "sound out" or use phonics concepts and skills to figure out a word he has never seen before (since he would never come across it while reading) strips away the memorized word bank and gives us a look at how he would approach an unknown word.

Decoding: using phonics knowledge to read; reading by "sounding out"

Encoding: using phonics knowledge to spell

Sample Graphic Organizers

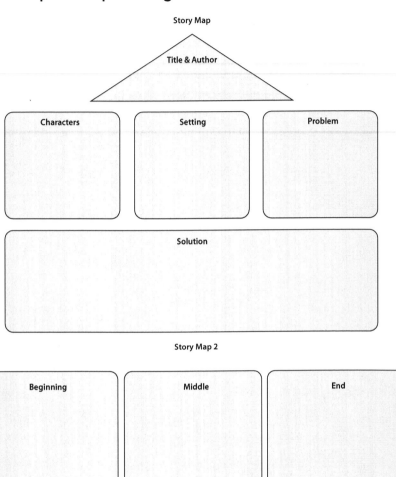

Story Map

Title & Author

| Characters | Setting | Problem |

Solution

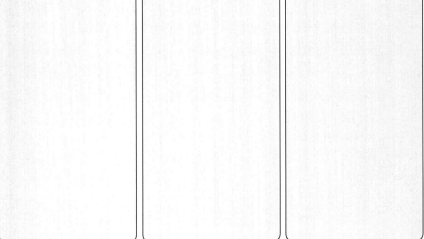

Story Map 2

| Beginning | Middle | End |

Prefix & Root

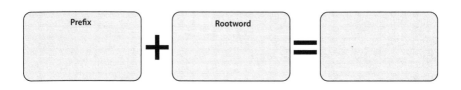

Prefix + Rootword =

Expository Text 1

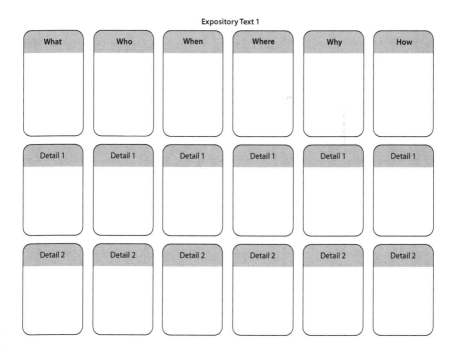

What	Who	When	Where	Why	How
Detail 1	Detail 1	Detail 1	Detail 1	Detail 1	Detail 1
Detail 2	Detail 2	Detail 2	Detail 2	Detail 2	Detail 2

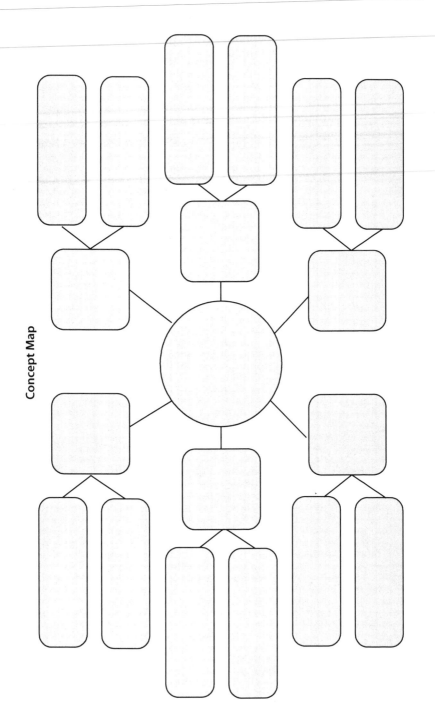

Concept Map

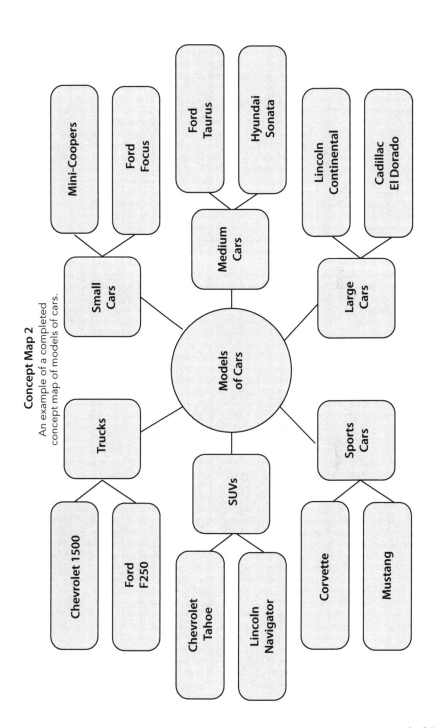

Concept Map 2

An example of a completed concept map of models of cars.

Cluster Web

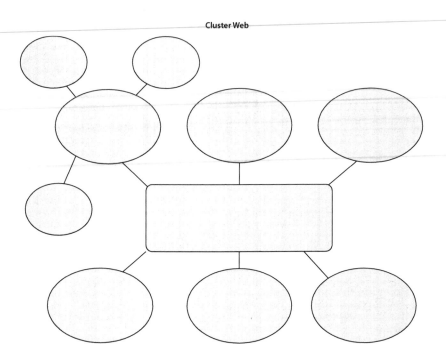

Heather Leneau Bragg, MA

Learning specialist and author, Heather Bragg, tutors young children who are struggling in elementary school and effectively coaches them into being better, happier students. Her background includes graduating with distinction from the University of Oklahoma with a bachelor's degree in Elementary Education. Initially, she taught first and third grades as a classroom teacher in Texas and Illinois. She wanted to know and practice the best teaching methods for all students but especially the young students who weren't doing as well as they could in school. This desire prompted her to earn a master's degree from Northwestern University in Communication Sciences and Disorders. Afterwards, she taught in the Chicago Public Schools system and later at the University of Chicago's Hyde Park Day School, a specialized school for children with mild-to-moderate language-based learning disabilities.

Heather works as a learning consultant and private tutor in the Chicago area. In those roles, and as a book author and speaker, she is spreading hopeful, practical advice and useful skill-building techniques for struggling young students and their parents and teachers. (As a parent herself, Heather reports that she continues to learn and grow daily!)

Web site is: **www.learningdecodedbook.com**

Learning Decoded: Understanding and Using Your Child's Unique Learning Style to Improve Academic Performance **is available on the web site and on Amazon.com.**

Patricia Alma Lee

Patricia Alma Lee, a Chicago author/editor and agent, is highly skilled at working with others to get their important stories written and promoted. She focuses on the personal growth and self-help genre. Books and e-books that she has coauthored or developmental edited include: "A Life Less Anxious," "Hey! Bartender!" "Speak Your Truth," and "Good Food, Better Life." She often works with top-tier physicians and businesspeople to create books, cds, and web sites. Multi-member team accomplishments have included such valuable clinical and financial products as: "Clinical Preventive Medicine" and other texts and the full range of Current Procedural Terminology products produced by the American Medical Association. She has developed content for several web sites and publications at the Feinberg School of Medicine at Northwestern University and the Rehabilitation Institute of Chicago.

After working with an Army combat physician to coauthor an Iraq War memoir, she started a memoir writing program at the Pritzker Military Library to coach veterans. The successful program was highlighted in the *Chicago Tribune.* She also wrote, produced, and starred in "A Soldier's Tale," a musical show based on her 94-year-old father's WW II experiences.

For a few years, Pat co-owned and operated "Call of the Sea," a nautical art gallery and gift store, at North Pier Chicago. Before that, she held progressively responsible positions as a human resources professional, primarily in compensation, for the first decade of her career.

A University of Illinois graduate, Pat also completed the University of Chicago's Publishing Program. Jazz singing is her favorite after-hours activity.